Manu's Ark

INDIA'S TALE *of the* GREAT FLOOD

Emma V. Moore

MANDALA
K I D S

San Rafael, California

$\mathcal{M}$any years ago in India, there lived a good and holy king. His name was Manu, Father of Man, for in his heart he cared about everyone and everything in the whole world.

Every day Manu went to the river and offered the great god Vishnu a handful of water as a way of thanking him for looking after the world. People had forgotten to care for the earth, and they had upset the balance of nature. Manu prayed for Vishnu to keep the world safe from harm.

One day, when Manu was offering water to Vishnu,
he noticed a tiny fish swimming in the palms of his
hands. Manu placed the fish back in the water. To his
surprise, the fish spoke.

"Would you leave me here to be eaten by bigger
fish?" said the fish. "Take me home."

Manu felt sorry for the little fish. He took him home and
placed him in a bowl. That night Manu dreamed he heard the
fish cry out for help.

When he woke up the next morning, Manu discovered that
the fish had grown too big for his bowl.

"Help me," said the fish. "Would you leave me here to die?"

Manu lifted the bowl and carried it outside to a well.
He tipped the fish into the well and turned to leave.
But the fish called out from the well, "Why have you
put me in this tiny well? I need more room to swim."

Manu peered into the well. To his astonishment the fish had grown again. Its large body pressed against the walls of the well, and its tail could barely move.

Manu lifted the large fish in his arms and carried it to the river. With a flick of its tail, the fish vanished in the deep water.

Breathing a sigh, Manu returned home. He was pleased
to have helped a creature in need. But that night he dreamed
that the fish once again called out for help.

The next morning Manu woke and went to his window. There he saw the most incredible sight. The fish had become so enormous that the river seemed like a shallow stream and the mountains behind looked like small hills.

The fish's eyes were wide and its fins flapped wildly. Its mouth opened and closed as though gasping for air. The fish thrashed about with such force that the ground shook.

Manu wondered what to do. Out of compassion he had rescued the fish, but the magical creature would not stop growing. With great difficulty, Manu guided the fish to the ocean. Once the fish was out of sight, Manu again breathed a sigh of relief and turned to leave.

At that moment a voice boomed as though from the heavens above. It was the fish, who said, "I need you once more."

When he heard this, Manu sat down in despair, his head in his hands. What more could he do to help the fish?

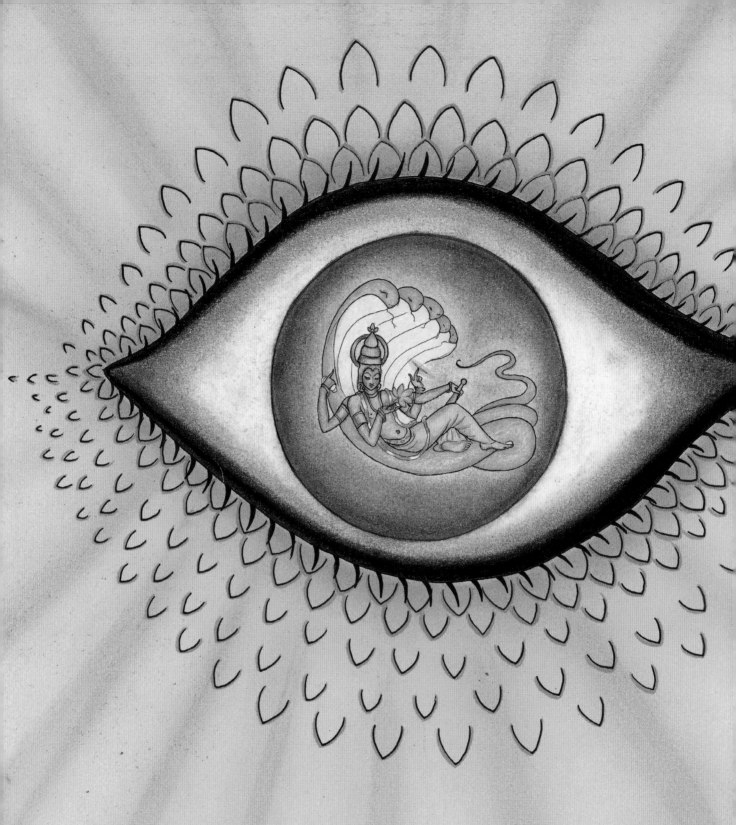

Manu looked out at the ocean and gasped. The fish was now the size of a mountain and gazing straight at him.

When Manu looked into one of the fish's giant eyes, he saw his beloved Lord Vishnu lying on a serpent bed. At last he understood. The fish was really Vishnu in the form of a fish.

"I am pleased with you," Vishnu said in a voice like thunder. "In this form I am known as Matsya. Because of your goodness, I have come to answer your prayer to keep the world safe from harm.

"Soon there will be a terrible flood, and the world will be covered by water. I will send you a boat. Collect two of every living thing in the world: humans, animals, and plants. Bring them all onto the boat.

"I will also send my great serpent. Use him as a rope to tie the boat to me."

After saying this Matsya swam away into the distance.

Manu gathered all the people, animals, and plants and brought them all onto the boat.

Soon the seas rolled and lightning flashed. The whole world was swallowed up in a raging storm.

The waters rose and the boat floated away, tossed this way and that by huge waves.

The people pleaded with Manu to bring them
to safety.

"Don't be afraid. I will look after you," said Manu.
But when he gazed at the stormy night sky he
wondered if Matsya had deserted him.

Suddenly, Matsya appeared in the distance like a
sun rising from the ocean. The waters parted as his
huge and graceful body swam toward Manu's boat.

Just as Matsya had promised,
a great serpent appeared.

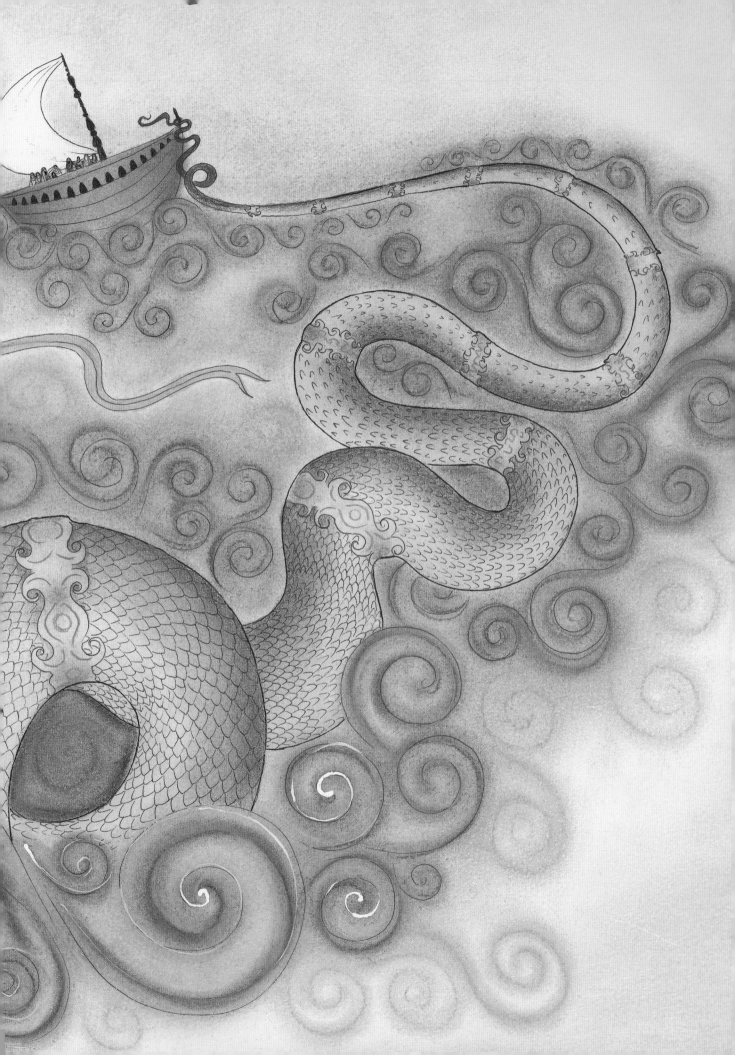

Matsya looked at Manu with eyes so large they seemed to extend from the churning depths below to the moon above. In those great eyes, Manu saw all the planets and stars. Even more amazing was the tear of gratitude that fell from one of Matsya's beautiful eyes. Manu wondered at the ways of the great god Vishnu.

For many years, the gigantic fish towed the
boat through stormy waters. The winds blew,
and the waves crashed.

But Manu and his companions remained safe aboard their boat.

At last the seas calmed. The darkness
dissolved and the sun rose. Fluffy white
clouds floated in a blue sky. The waters
gradually receded, and Manu's boat
came to rest on a sandy shore.

Manu led the people and animals
from his boat onto the dry land.
At last they were safe.

Manu remembered the day he found Matsya, a tiny fish, swimming in the palms of his hands. He thought of the great flood and of the years he had spent adrift in a long and terrible storm.

Manu kneeled down by the water's edge. He took a handful of water in his palms and raised them to the sky. With a heart full of wonder and devotion, he offered it to the great god Vishnu.

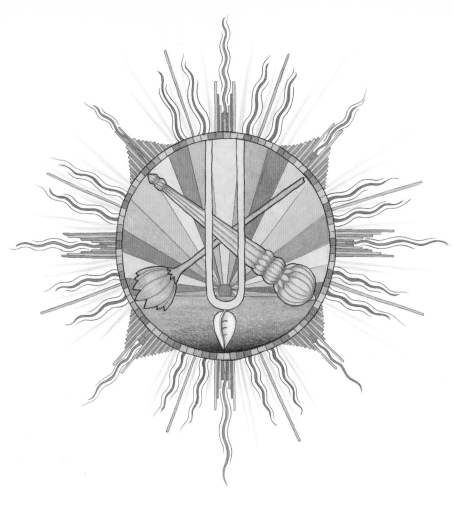

MANDALA
K I D S

PO Box 3088
San Rafael, CA 94912
www.mandalapublishing.com

Text and illustrations copyright © 2012 by Emma V. Moore
emmavmoore.co.uk

Illustrations were created using pastels and watercolor crayons.

Library of Congress Cataloging-in-Publication Data available.

ISBN: 978-1-60887-092-9

REPLANTED PAPER

Insight Editions, in association with Roots of Peace, will plant two
trees for each tree used in the manufacturing of this book. Roots of
ROOTS of PEACE Peace is an internationally renowned humanitarian organization
dedicated to eradicating land mines worldwide and converting war-torn
lands into productive farms and wildlife habitats. Together, we will plant
two million fruit and nut trees in Afghanistan and provide farmers there
with the skills and support necessary for sustainable land use.

Manufactured in China by Insight Editions

10 9 8 7 6 5 4 3 2 1